Robots

KINGFISHER
LONDON & NEW YORK

Distributed in the U.S. and Canada by Macmillan, 175 Fifth Ave., New York, NY 10010

First published as *Kingfisher Young Knowledge: Robots* in 2003
Additional material produced for Kingfisher by Discovery Books Ltd.

Library of Congress Cataloging-in-Publication data has been applied for.

ISBN: 978-0-7534-6607-0

Kingfisher books are available for special promotions and premiums.
For details contact: Special Markets Department, Macmillan, 175 Fifth Ave., New York, NY 10010.

For more information, please visit www.kingfisherbooks.com

Printed in China
3 5 7 9 8 6 4 2

2TR/0312/WKT/UG/140MA

Note to readers: the website addresses listed in this book are correct at the time of going to print. However, due to the ever-changing nature of the Internet, website addresses and content can change. Websites can contain links that are unsuitable for children. The publisher cannot be held responsible for changes in website addresses or content or for information obtained through a third party. We strongly advise that Internet searches be supervised by an adult.

Acknowledgments
The publisher would like to thank the following for permission to reproduce their material. Every care has been taken to trace copyright holders. However, if there have been unintentional omissions or failure to trace copyright holders, we apologize and will, if informed, endeavor to make corrections in any future edition.
b = bottom, *c* = center, *l* = left, *t* = top, *r* = right

Photographs: *cover*: Shutterstock Images; 6–7 *c* Sony/SDR-4X; 8–9 *l* Getty Images; *c* eMuu, Dr. Christoph Bartneck, Technical University of Eindhoven; *br* Peter Menzel/Science Photo Library; 10–11 *bl* James King-Holmes/Science Photo Library, *br* Photo: (Ingrid Friedl) Lufthansa Technik Skywash/Lufthansa, Putzmeister AG; *tr* Space and Naval Warfare Systems Center, San Diego; 12–13 *cl* © Randy Montoya, Sandia National Laboratories; *c* Robosaurus/Doug Malewicki, Monster Robot Inc., *tr* Coneyl Jay/Science Photo Library; 14–15 *bl* Honda Asimo; *tr* Eriko Fugita/Reuters/Popperfoto; *c* Sam Ogden/Science Photo Library; 16–17 *bl* Sony/AIBO ERS-220; *tr* © Dr. Gavin Miller SnakeRobots.com, Copyright 2000; *r* BBH Exhibits Inc./Oscar Williams; 18–19 *cl* Richard Bachmann, Gabriel Nelson and Roger Quinn at Case Western Reserve University; *bc* MIT, Bruce Frisch/Science Photo Library; *tr* Sarcos; 20–21 *tr* PA photos/Sony; *br* PA photos; *tr, bl* TM Robotics (Europe) Ltd./Toshiba; 22–23 *bc* Associated Press; *bl* MIT Media Lab, Getty Images; *tr* NASA/Carnegie Mellon University, Science Photo Library; 24–25 *bl* modelluboot@t-online.de (Norbert Brüggen); *c* Getty Images; *tr* Associated Press; 26–27 *bl* NASA/Science Photo Library; *tr* NASA/Science Photo Library; *br* Media Resource Center NASA/ Lyndon B. Johnson Space Center; 28–29 *tr* Courtesy of the School of Mechanical Engineering, The University of Western Australia; *b* Louisianna State University; *cr* © Ron Sanford/CORBIS; *tl* Digital Vision; 30–31 *tc* PaPeRo/© NEC Corporation 2001–2003; *cl* © Roger Ressmeyer/Corbis; *br* Electric handout/ Reuters/Popperfoto; 32–33 *bl* Spencer Grant/Science Photo Library; *br* Roy Garner/Rex Features; *tr* CRASAR™/www.crasar.org; 34–35 *bl* Associated Press; *c* © Cynthia's Bar and Restaurant; *tr* Associated Press; 36–37 *bc* Peter Menzel/Science Photo Library; *cl r* AeroVironment Inc.; *tr* www.edwards.af/Edwards Air Force Base; 38–39 Peter Menzel/Science Photo Library; 40–41 *bl* Tri-Star for *Short Circuit*/Kobal; *bl* Sautelet, Jerrican/Science Photo Library; *tr* AAR Productions/Kobal. *Short Circuit* Tri-Star Pictures; *Return of the Jedi* Lucasfilm; *Doctor Who* BBC TV; 48*t* Shutterstock Images/Gemenacon; 48*b* NASA/courtesy of nasaimages.org; 49 BigDog image provided courtesy of Boston Dynamics ©2009; 52*t* Shutterstock Images/Baloncici; 52*b* Shutterstock Images/DenisKlimov; 53 Shutterstock Images/Small Town Studio; 56 Shutterstock Images/DenisKlimov

Commissioned photography on pages 42–47 by Andy Crawford
Thank you to models Eleanor Davis, Lewis Manu, Daniel Newton, Lucy Newton, Nikolas Omilana, and Olivia Omilana

Robots

Clive Gifford

KINGFISHER
NEW YORK

Contents

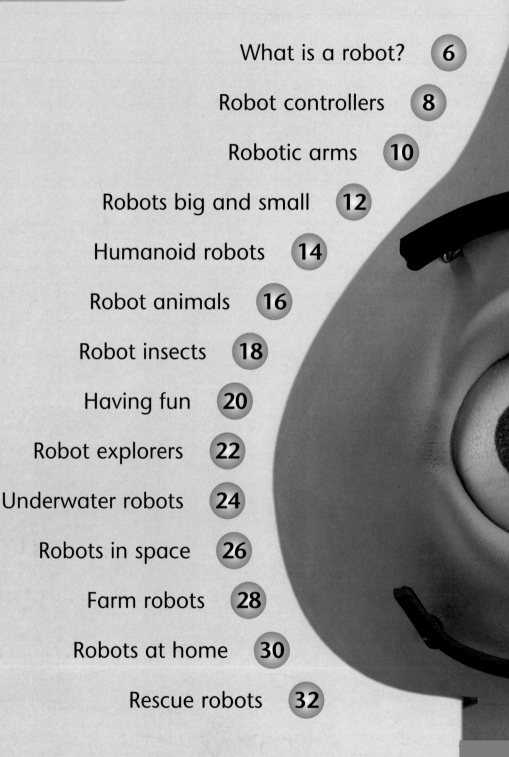

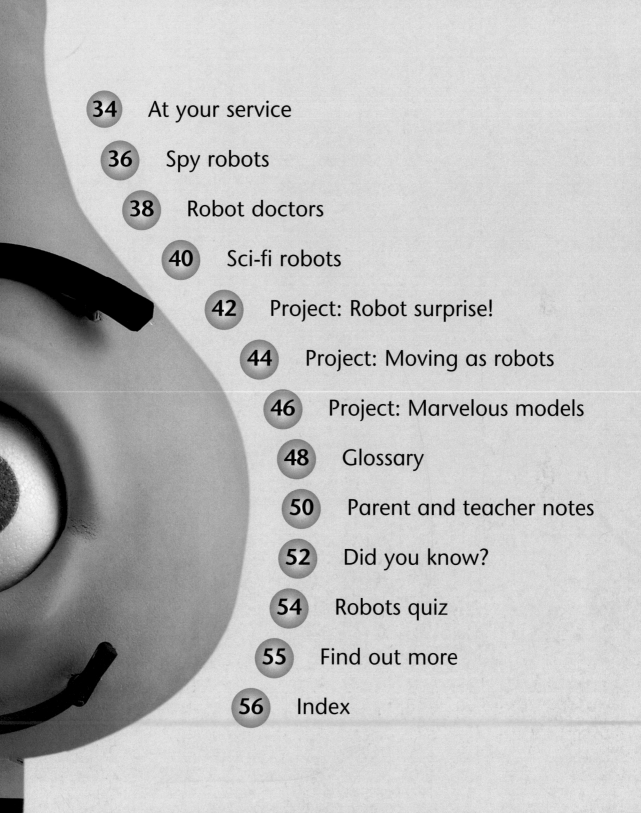

What is a robot?

Robots are amazing machines that can work on their own. They can go into many places— from outer space to deep underwater.

Eyes, ears, mouth
Robots collect information about the world using devices called sensors. This Sony robot has sensors that record sound and cameras that capture pictures.

Handy workers

Robots can often do more than one job. Gripping hands allow them to hold and use many different tools and objects.

On the move

Many robots move using legs, wheels, or caterpillar tracks (like the ones on tanks). This robot has knee and hip joints that work just like human knees and hips.

Robot controllers

Controllers are a robot's brain. They make decisions for the robot and operate all of its parts. Robot controllers are usually computers.

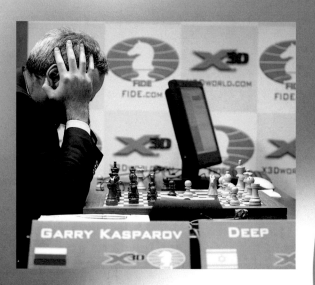

GARRY KASPAROV   DEEP

Fast thinkers

Computers make decisions very quickly. *Deep Junior* can think through three million chess moves every second. Here, it is playing against the former World Chess champion, Garry Kasparov.

Showing emotion

This robot is named *eMuu*. It interacts with people and can show many different expressions, including happiness, anger, and sadness.

Learning to walk

Some robots are controlled by people. Others are autonomous, or able to work by themselves. This autonomous robot from Japan is teaching itself to walk.

Robotic **arms**

Robotic arms are the most popular type of robot. They have joints so that the arm can move in many different directions, just like a human arm.

Get a grip!

Many robotic arms end with a robotic hand, called a gripper. Grippers are often fitted with pressure sensors to help judge how much force is needed to grip a particular object.

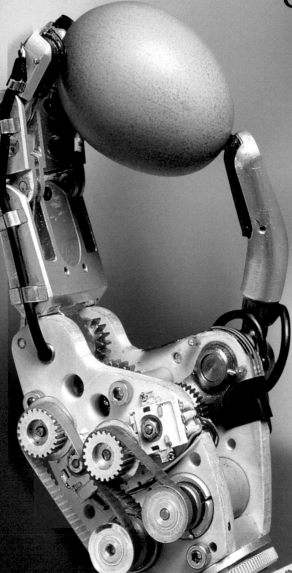

Robot guards

This robot security guard seeks out intruders. Its left arm carries a rangefinder. Its right arm controls a gun that can fire darts.

Jet wash

Skywash, a giant robotic arm, cleans jumbo jets in record time. It takes about three hours to wash an airplane. Without this robot, it could take up to 12 hours.

Robots big and small

Robots come in many shapes and sizes. The largest are many feet high and weigh thousands of pounds. Different-size robots use different power systems to move their parts.

Mighty monster

Robosaurus is a car-crushing monster. It uses hydraulic power (the power of liquids) to lift and destroy cars, trucks, and even airplanes!

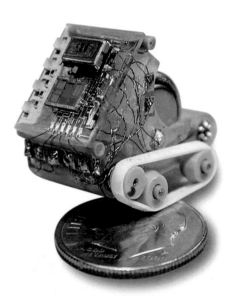

Marvelous *MARV*

MARV is a moving robot that is so small, it can sit on a coin! Its tiny electric motor is powered by watch batteries. *MARV* moves at a speed of only 20 inches (50 centimeters) per minute.

Shrinking small

One day, robots may become so small that they will be able to travel inside our bodies! Robots might even travel through our veins, cleaning and repairing them.

14 Humanoid robots

People are fascinated by machines that look and act just like them. Scientists are building humanoid robots that can perform a wide range of skills.

Stair walkers

Scientists have figured out how to keep a two-legged robot upright when it walks. Honda's *Asimo* robot can even go up and down stairs with ease.

Want a ride?

This humanoid robot from Asia acts as a ricksha driver, pulling people around. It is powered by motors in its head and chest.

Show your feelings

Kismet is one of the few robots able to show facial expressions. Its mouth, eyelids, eyebrows, and eyes all move to show expressions such as fear, happiness, disgust, interest, and surprise.

Robot animals

Some robots are made to look like animals. This might be to make an exhibition more fun or to make moving models for movies. Scientists also borrow ideas from animals to make robots move smoothly.

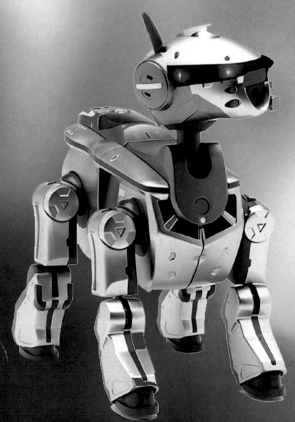

Snakes alive
Snakes move by sliding their bodies across the ground. This robot *S5* snake can slide through pipes and other cramped spaces.

A new best friend
Sony's *AIBO ERS-220* is a mobile robot that has been programmed to behave like a dog. It recognizes 75 different words and will respond to its owner calling out its name.

Standing tall

This robot giraffe uses parts of machines to show how the parts of real animals work. It looks down on visitors at the Robot Zoo exhibition on its world tours.

Robot insects

Insects are very successful creatures that can live in many different places. Robot makers have copied some insects in order to build robots that can work in extreme conditions.

Robo-roach!

Ajax is designed to look like a cockroach. Each of its front legs has five joints, and the robot can stay balanced on just three of its six legs.

Flying insects

This model of a monarch butterfly flaps its wings using "muscle" wires. These wires shorten in length when electricity is applied.

Creepy-crawler!

Genghis was one of the first insect robots to be built. Its six legs allow it to move over uneven ground. When it comes across something too big to climb over, *Genghis* simply backs away and chooses another route.

Having fun

Playing sports is a lot of fun for people, but for robots it is a big test of their abilities. Robots need to be able to make quick decisions and to move their parts rapidly in order to play sports.

Playing volleyball
These Japanese test robots are learning to play volleyball. Each robot uses cameras to track the path of the ball and times the movement of its joints to meet the ball in midair.

Goal!

Balancing on one foot, this *Sony SDR-3X* robot moves its leg joints to kick a ball toward a goal. Although it is fast for a robot, people can move 20 times more quickly.

World Cup for robots

These robots are playing in RoboCup, a worldwide soccer competition for moving robots. They use sensors to know where the ball is and where their teammates are.

Robot explorers

Robots can be built to explore places that are too dangerous for people to visit. They can take pictures and send back useful information without putting people at risk.

Robo reporter

This test robot, named *Afghan Explorer*, may one day visit war zones. Working as a war reporter, it could send back pictures and interviews to a TV studio in a safer location.

Into the volcano

This eight-legged robot is named *Dante II*. It can climb into the crater of a red-hot volcano to collect gas samples and take photos with its eight cameras.

Hot and cold worker

Nomad Rover is the size of a small car. It has trekked through hot deserts and icy lands all on its own, collecting information for scientists back home. In Antarctica, it discovered five meteorites.

Underwater robots

Many robots work underwater. They map out the ocean floor, monitor sealife, or find sunken shipwrecks. Robots can travel deep underwater far more easily than people can.

Unmanned submarine
Robots can stay underwater for many days at a time. They can travel hundreds of miles exploring the oceans.

Deep-sea explorer

Robots such as *Deep Drone* can travel to the ocean floor and help recover crashed aircraft or sunken ships. *Deep Drone* can travel about 40 times deeper than unprotected human divers can.

Robot jellyfish

Some underwater robots are modeled on real sea creatures. This robot jellyfish has a small electric motor that makes it rise and fall in the water just like a real jellyfish.

Robots in space

Astronauts need special equipment for surviving in space. Robots do not need air, water, or food. They can work on distant planets, staying in touch with Earth by use of radio signals.

Photos in space

AERCam Sprint robot can zoom around the outside of a space shuttle or a space station. The beachball-size robot sends back images to the astronauts inside the spacecraft.

Robot astronauts

Robonaut is a test robot built by NASA to work as a construction worker in space. It has two robotic arms that can grip and use a range of tools.

Mission to Mars

NASA's *Sojourner Rover* was the very first robot to travel across part of another planet. In 1997, the six-wheeled rover explored part of the surface of Mars.

Farm robots

Farming is hard work. Robots can help by doing some of the boring tasks that take up time. Farm robots can handle small plants, help at harvests, or scare away pests.

Chasing birds
Scarebot is a robot that patrols catfish ponds in the United States. Its sudden movements scare away pelicans and other birds hoping for a fish snack!

Shear magic!

This robot from Australia has been programmed to shear the wool off a sheep. It can keep repeating the task without getting tired.

Robots at home

Robots are coming home. The latest robots are doing useful jobs around the house. Home robots need to know their way around a house and be able to communicate with their owners.

Ready for breakfast?

Robots cannot cook your meals yet, but they can carry them to you. Home robots often hold a map of the house in their memory. They also need sensors in order to know when household objects are in their way.

Home playmates

PaPeRos wander around the house looking for people to talk to. They can recognize 650 different words and phrases and speak up to 3,000 words. They can even dance!

Beware of the dog

This robot guard dog patrols the house, checking that everything is safe. If it spots anything wrong, it can take pictures and send them to the owner's cell phone.

Rescue robots

Some robots can save lives. They do this by fighting fires, searching for survivors after disasters, or handling dangerous objects such as unexploded bombs.

Handling bombs

Bomb-disposal robots can look at suspect packages with their cameras. They then relay the information to someone at a safe distance.

SEP 15 2001
11:25:01 PM

Access all areas

Packbot enters unknown areas to check for danger. After the 2001 terrorist attack, *Packbot* searched the wreckage of the World Trade Center in New York for survivors.

Fighting fires

Robots can cope with much higher temperatures than people can, and they do not need air to breathe. This makes them excellent firefighters that can get in close to put out a blaze.

At your service

Service robots are able to perform useful, repetitive, everyday tasks for people. They are willing workers and do not get bored when doing simple jobs over and over again.

Fill her up!

Filling up your car with gas can be a hassle, but not for this robot attendant. Its robotic arm can find a car's gas tank and fill it up with the amount of gas that the driver chooses.

Carry your bag?

The *Intelecady* carries a bag of golf clubs around a golf course. The robot has a map of the course in its memory so that it can avoid any bunkers or streams.

Drinks please

Cynthia is a robot bartender at work in London, England. *Cynthia's* robotic arms can select, grip, and pour ingredients from bottles to mix customers one of 60 different drinks.

Spy robots

Human spies must be intelligent and sneaky. But robots can be built to get into places that humans cannot and send back information using radio signals. If spy robots are caught, they will not give away any secrets.

Mini spy

Smaller robots can travel into places without being spotted. This flying robot is only 6 inches (15 centimeters) wide. It can fly for 30 minutes, powered by a tiny engine.

Hovering above

Cypher is a 6-foot (2-meter)-wide robot that can hover outside the windows of tall buildings. It can look and listen in on top-secret meetings using microphones and cameras.

Watching you?

Roswell is a robot with 16 different sensors. Future spy robots may be able to identify people and follow them.

Robot doctors

Robots can work accurately for hours without making an error or getting tired. They make ideal assistants for human surgeons in hospital operations.

A steady hand

A human surgeon controls the *Da Vinci* robot while studying a magnified view of the operation. The robot's arms are fitted with surgical tools that perform the operation.

Sci-fi robots

Long before real robots were made, they were popular in science-fiction books and movies. Many sci-fi robots have incredible powers and are often shown fighting to take over the world!

Short Circuit
This robot is *No. 5*, the star of the movie *Short Circuit*. In the movie, *No. 5* was built as a robot weapon, but after being struck by lightning, it refused to fight and started to learn and think for itself.

Exterminate!

Many sci-fi robots are shown as evil, including this *Dalek* from the British TV show *Doctor Who*. Real robots are programmed by people, so they are only as dangerous as people make them.

Robot actors

This animatronic model of Yoda is from the movie *Return of the Jedi*, part of the *Star Wars* series. Its many electric motors allow it to make realistic movements.

Robot surprise!

Make a secret storage robot

Robots are super-organized and find information very quickly. This robust robot storage box will help you find your treasures whenever you need them—and also keep your bedroom tidy!

You will need:
- Shoebox
- Small box
- Poster paints
- Paintbrush
- Scissors
- Cleaning cloth
- Glue and paintbrush
- Cardboard tubes
- Candy wrappers
- Ping-Pong balls
- Double-sided tape
- Pipe cleaners

1

Paint the boxes and cardboard tubes and leave to dry. Carefully cut off the two shorter ends of the shoebox lid along the fold line.

2

Using glue or double-sided tape, attach one edge of the lid to the shoebox and press it down firmly. Cut two hand shapes from the cleaning cloth and wrap a candy wrapper or piece of colored paper around the Ping-Pong ball.

3

Use the smaller box as the robot's head and decorate it with pipe cleaners. Cut the long cardboard tube in half and glue one cloth hand on each. Stick these onto the sides of the shoebox. Glue the other tubes on as feet and the wrapped ball as a handle.

Moving as robots

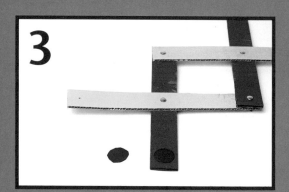

Make a moving arm

Robots can be programmed to perform many tasks. They can pick up things and move them around. This arm can pick up paper clips.

Using the scissors, carefully cut the cardboard into strips. All of the strips need to be the same length and width.

You will need:
- Scissors
- 2 large sheets of cardboard
- Paper fasteners and clips
- Double-sided tape or glue
- 2 small magnets

Make a crossover lattice of strips and join it together with the paper fasteners. You will need to use a paper fastener in the middle of each strip, as well as at the ends.

Take two small magnets and attach them to one end of the arm. By opening and closing the other end, you can use the arm to pick up paper clips.

Walk like a robot

Very few robots can actually think for themselves. Most have to follow instructions. When you walk, your eyes show you where obstacles are and your brain figures out how to avoid them. Here, you can learn how to move like a robot, just by following instructions.

Ask a friend to help you set up a maze using furniture. Find a blindfold or close your eyes—but no peeking! Ask your friend to tell you how to walk through the maze without bumping into things. If the directions are wrong, you will hit the furniture!

Marvelous models

Make a model robot

Robots come in many shapes and sizes. Make a model robot out of empty cartons and boxes from your home. It can be any shape or size you want.

You will need:
- Boxes
- Ping-Pong balls
- Plastic cups
- Scissors
- Glue and brush
- Cardboard tubes
- Tinfoil
- Carton lid
- Pipe cleaners
- Thin cardboard
- Candy wrappers
- Colored paper
- Tape

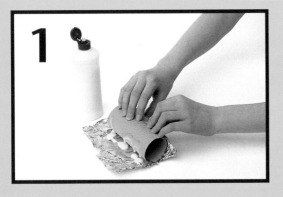

Using glue, carefully stick tinfoil around four of the cardboard tubes and the boxes.

Cover another cardboard tube with colored paper and carefully cut into the ends so that they will sit flat.

Glue candy wrappers or colored paper onto a carton lid and then stick it to the big box.

Attach plastic cups to one end of the big box. Stick a piece of cardboard to the bottoms of them (as a stand).

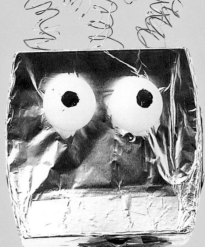

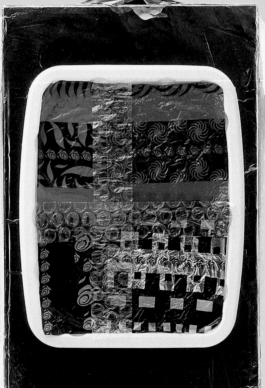

Decorate the smaller box with painted Ping-Pong balls and pipe cleaners. Stick the arms onto your robot.

Open out the cut ends of the decorated cardboard tube and attach it to the head and body.

Glossary

animatronic—describes a model that uses computers and robotics to bring it to life

astronaut—a person who travels into outer space

autonomous—working independently of others

battery—a device that stores electricity

caterpillar track—a metal belt that is stretched around a set of wheels, helping vehicles travel over rough ground

cockroach—an insect that often lives in houses

communicate—to send or receive a message

humanoid—looking or acting like a person

hydraulic—operated by a fluid under pressure

interview—a meeting where someone is asked questions

magnified—made to look bigger

meteorite—a piece of rock or metal that has fallen to Earth from space

monitor—to check the condition of something

muscle—a part of an animal's body that helps it move

NASA—short name for the National Aeronautics and Space Administration, the United States space agency

programmed—given a list of instructions to perform

repetitive—describes something that is done over and over

reporter—someone who collects and writes news stories for a newspaper or magazine

security guard—a person who looks after a building

sensor—a device that gives a robot information about its surroundings

space shuttle—a reusable spacecraft that takes off like a rocket but lands like a plane

spy—someone who gathers secrets about other countries

suspect—something that may be wrong or dangerous

tank—an armored vehicle used by the armed forces

terrorist—describes someone who commits violent acts for religious or political reasons

unmanned—without people on board

vein—one of a number of long tubes in which blood is carried around the body

The content of this book will be useful to teach, reinforce, and enhance various elements of the science and language arts curricula. It also provides opportunities for crosscurricular connections in design, geography, art, and math.

Extension activities

Writing
1) If you were to design an animal robot (pp. 16–17), which animal would you choose? Describe your robot and the types of things that it would be able to do.

2) Write a science-fiction story involving robots and humans or some other life form on planet Earth.

Writing and oral language
1) You are a sportscaster at the World Volleyball Tournament finals between a human team and a robot team. Write what you might say as you describe the last three minutes of tiebreaker play at the end of the game. Read it aloud as if you were a sportscaster (p. 20).

2) If your robot could only speak 20 words, which ones would you choose? Try them out to see if you can have a conversation using them (p. 31).

Science
The topic of robots relates to the themes of scientific inquiry, technological design, inventions, and structure and function.

Crosscurricular links
1) *Geography, writing and art:* If you were to use a robot to explore any place on Earth or elsewhere, where would you send it? What would you like it to find out? What types of things would you want it to do? Write about your robot and illustrate it in its environment.

2) *Writing, design, art, and oral language:* Design a robot to do your least-favorite chore (p. 30). Describe what it looks like, what it does, how you would communicate with it, and why it would do the job better than you do!

3) *Math and graphic organization:* Use a Venn diagram to show what a robot can do that a human can't, what a human can do that a robot can't, and what they both can do.

Using the projects
Children can follow or adapt these projects at home. Here are some ideas for extending them:

Page 42: At night, while you are asleep, your secret storage robot goes off on its own. Where does it go? What does it do? Create a series of booklets about the adventures of the Secret Storage Robot.

Page 44: Sit at a table blindfolded. Bend your arm at the elbow and rest it on the table, but keep it stiff. Ask a friend to place a small object somewhere on the table within reach. Have your friend use words to direct your hand and arm toward the object by telling you how far to move your arm, which direction, which joint to bend and how much, etc., until you reach the object.

Page 46: Think about how you would program your robot so that it could move and follow commands. What would you have it do? How would you control it?

Did you know?

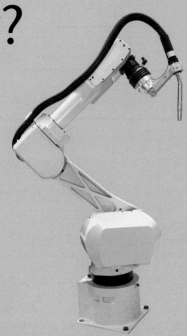

- There are 6.5 million robots in use throughout the world. Thirty percent of them are in Japan.

- The word *robot* comes from the Czech word *robota*, which means "forced work or labor."

- An android is a robot shaped like a human being.

- The first designs for a humanoid robot were made in the 1500s by the famous architect, artist, and inventor Leonardo da Vinci.

- The first humanoid robot was named *Elektro*. Built in 1939, it could speak 700 words.

- The first computer-controlled hand was developed in 1961 at the Massachusetts Institute of Technology in the United States.

- Humans have five senses: touch, taste, sight, smell, and hearing. The most advanced robots have at least two—sight and touch.

- Honda's humanoid robot *Asimo* cost an estimated $1 million to make.

- Almost all unmanned space probes are robots.

- The Mars Exploration Rover *Opportunity* has been traveling around Mars since 2004, sending back pictures and other information about the red planet.

- The first industrial robot, named *Unimate*, was used in 1961 by the American car manufacturer General Motors.

- The world's strongest industrial robot is the *Kuka KR1000 Titan*. It can lift loads that weigh up to 1.1 ton (1 metric tonne).

- The smallest humanoid robot in the world is the *Be-Robot*. It is only 6 inches (153 millimeters) tall.

- The underwater exploration robot *Deep Drone* can travel to depths of up to 8,200 feet (2,500 meters).

Robots quiz

The answers to these questions can all be found by looking back through the book. See how many you get right. You can check your answers on page 56.

1) How many chess moves can *Deep Junior* think through in one second?
A—30
B—3,000
C—3 million

2) How long does it take *Skywash* to clean a jumbo jet?
A—3 hours
B—13 hours
C—30 hours

3) Which was the first robot to travel across part of another planet?
A—*AERCam Sprint*
B—*Nomad Rover*
C—*Sojourner Rover*

4) How do robots collect information?
A—they use their sensors
B—they read books
C—they ask their friends

5) How fast can *MARV* move?
A—30 miles (50 kilometers) per hour
B—20 inches (50 centimeters) per minute
C—20 inches (50 centimeters) per second

6) How many words can Sony's *AIBO ERS-220* recognize?
A—7
B—27
C—75

7) What is the robot *Ajax* designed to look like?
A—a cockroach
B—a chicken
C—a cat

8) What task does the robot *Dante II* perform?
A—it measures rainfall
B—it collects gas samples in volcanoes
C—it dives deep into the sea

9) How many words can *PaPeRo*s speak?
A—30
B—300
C—3,000

10) What type of robot is the *Da Vinci* robot?
A—a military robot
B—a surgical robot
C—an exploration robot

11) Which activity is Honda's *Asimo robot* designed to perform?
A—walk up stairs
B—rollerskate
C—vacuum a house

12) Why did the robot *No. 5* stop fighting in the movie *Short Circuit*?
A—he was struck by lightning
B—he fell in love
C—he was reprogrammed

Find out more

Books to read

Robots and Artificial Intelligence (The Technology Behind) by Nicolas Brasch, Smart Apple Media, 2011

Robots & Rovers (Xtreme Space) by Sue L. Hamilton, Abdo & Daughters, 2011

Robots by Steve Weston, Kingfisher, 2010

Robots for Work and Fun (Robot World) by Steve Parker, Amicus, 2011

Robots in Dangerous Places (Robot World) by Steve Parker, Franklin Watts, 2010

Science Kids: Robots by Clive Gifford, Kingfisher, 2007

Places to visit

The Museum of Springfield History, Springfield, Massachusetts
http://robotstour.com/index.html
A fun and educational exhibit exploring the mechanical world—hosted by characters from the movie *Robots*. See how robots are improving our lives and even build your own robot.

Carnegie Science Center, Pittsburgh, Pennysylvania
www.visitroboworld.com/visitroboworld/index.aspx
Roboworld is the world's largest permanent robot exhibition. Get behind the scenes with interactive stations and learn how robots function.

Museum of Science and Industry, Chicago, Illinois
www.msichicago.org/whats-here/exhibits/toymaker/
Toymaker 3000: An Adventure in Automation is a fun, interactive exhibition for children and adults alike. Watch as a toy goes through the entire manufacturing process, from start to finish.

Websites

Honda—*Asimo*
www.world.honda.com/ASIMO/
Learn all there is to know about *Asimo*, the walking robot on the official website.

A Brief History of Robotics
http://robotics.megagiant.com/history.html
A timeline of robotics, from an ancient Greek mechanical pigeon to the Mars Exploration Rover.

How to make your own nanorover
http://spaceplace.jpl.nasa.gov/en/kids/muses2.shtml
How to make your own robotic vehicle using everyday items such as food trays, paper clips, balloons, and rubber bands.

Robots quiz answers

1) C   7) A
2) A   8) B
3) C   9) C
4) A   10) B
5) B   11) A
6) C   12) A